JAZZ MASTERS

Art Tatum

JAZZ MASTERS

Art Tatum

by Jed Distler

Amsco Publications
New York/London/Sydney

ACKNOWLEDGEMENTS

I would like to thank Clifford Jay Safane for his help in getting this project off the ground
and contributing research material, as well as Gary Giddens and Felicity Howlett
for providing recordings and vital information. Most of all, I thank two exceptional musicians and friends,
Dick Hyman and Andrew Thomas. Their insights and suggestions were invaluable to me in my work.

Edited by Patricia Ann Neely
Cover design by Barbara Hoffman
Book design by Tina Cernano
Cover photo by Robert Parent

Copyright © 1981 by Consolidated Music Publishers,
This book published 1986 by Amsco Publications,
A Division of Music Sales Corporation, New York, NY.

Order No. AM 30719
International Standard Book Number: 0.8256.4085.7

Exclusive Distributors:
Music Sales Corporation
257 Park Avenue South, New York, NY 10010 USA
Music Sales Limited
8/9 Frith Street, London W1V 5TZ England
Music Sales Pty. Limited
120 Rothschild Street, Rosebery, Sydney, NSW 2018, Australia

Printed in the United States of America by
Vicks Lithograph and Printing Corporation

Contents

Art Tatum

(1910-1956)

Art Tatum was born October 13th, 1910 in Toledo, Ohio, totally blind in one eye and with only slight vision in the other. He studied the violin for two years and then changed over to the piano when he was about fourteen years old. Within a few years, Tatum had made incredible progress, establishing an unprecedented degree of pianistic control and maturity for a teenager.

At eighteen Tatum became staff pianist on a Toledo radio station, WSPD. As "Arthur Tatum, Toledo's blind pianist," he played background music for Ellen Kay's daily shopping chat program. Tatum first came to New York in 1932 as an accompanist for singer Adelaide Hall and it was with her that he made his first recordings. He cut his first solo record, "Tiger Rag," on August 5th, 1932.

Tatum worked primarily in nightclubs throughout the 30s. He led a small band for a long run at the Three Deuces in Chicago and played at the legendary Onyx Club in New York. In late 1937 he embarked on a small European tour. His first major concert appearance, however, was with a band consisting of the winners of the first annual *Esquire* poll at the Metropolitan Opera House in January, 1944. The concert was recorded in its entirety (on Radiola 2MR-5051) and is a rare and instructive example of Tatum successfully working with his peers in a live performance. Tatum also placed first in the 1945 *Metronome Readers' Poll* and in the *Down Beat Critics' Poll* from 1954 to 1956.

After 1945 Tatum began to play jazz concerts regularly, although he still made frequent nightclub appearances as a solo artist and with his trio. Tatum died of uremia on November 4th, 1956, in Los Angeles. Almost twenty-five years after his death and with the significant developments in jazz piano, Art Tatum's music still remains the standard by which the mainstream of jazz solo piano is measured.

The Art Tatum Style

Art Tatum made his first commercial solo piano recordings in 1932 and 1933. These records, along with an existing 1934 aircheck, show an accomplished virtuoso steeped in the roots of Fats Waller and Lee Sims, two pianists who made deep impressions upon the young Tatum. Lee Sims was a "pop" pianist who often used arpeggios, runs, and extended harmonic structures to embellish the melodies he used. The Waller influence, however, has a greater bearing on Tatum's style in terms of his left-hand conception and his overall sense of swing. Like Waller, Tatum often "strides in tenths" (the left hand using patterns alternating tenths in the bass register with full chords in the middle register) and also like Waller, seldom uses the hemiola or *drop-bass* left-hand patterns developed by James P. Johnson and Willie "The Lion" Smith. From a musical standpoint these recordings are fascinating and overwhelming. The young Art Tatum shows off his technique, frequently destroying the momentum of a ballad by suddenly falling into very fast stride tempos and embroidering his naturally swinging melodic phrases with glib arpeggios. The overall importance of these recordings lies in their awesome pianistic authority and control. Even at breakneck tempos Tatum managed to sound completely relaxed and at ease.

Between 1934 and 1941 Tatum recorded many solos for the Brunswick and Decca labels (reissued in the United States by MCA). These sessions include his most famous, and probably definitive, versions of such standards as "Tea for Two," "Tiger Rag," "Get Happy," "Sweet Lorraine," "Elegie," and "Humoresque." All the facets of his style have become more focused. He uses runs and arpeggios more discreetly and the pianistic textures are both transparent and yet full bodied.

The first recordings of the Art Tatum Trio appeared in 1943. The clever ensemble arrangements and often humorous interplay between Tatum, guitarist Tiny Grimes, and bassist Slam Stewart added to the group's popularity. Although the trio was a tempting format for displaying the flashy side of his talent Tatum could, and often did, deliver driving, non-stop, linear improvisations that hinted at what Bud Powell would be doing in the late 40s and what Oscar Peterson would do very soon after. He worked on and off in a trio setting until shortly before his death in 1956.

Tatum recorded sporadically from 1945 to the middle of 1949. His recordings from the latter part of that year, however, reveal significant musical growth and are important in comparison to his subsequent recordings. His playing on the three solo sessions for Capitol and on the Columbia LP recorded in concert is richly textured, rhythmically adventurous, and sophisticated harmonically. The role of the left hand has increased considerably; Tatum's bass lines are more adventurous, frequently using walking left-hand chords with tenths as the outside interval. (This is particularly significant since the bop pianists who were coming of age left their left hands at home, with the notable exceptions of George Shearing, Dave McKenna, and Hank Jones.) Tatum's left hand frequently breaks away from its accompanying role and becomes an equal partner with the right hand, sharing roles and embellishments and providing countermelodies. This musical development can be observed in the transcriptions in this volume. (Compare, for example, "Ain't Misbehavin' " with "Moonglow" or the two versions of "Sweet Lorraine."

Between December, 1953 and January, 1955 Tatum recorded four marathon solo piano sessions for jazz producer and entrepreneur Norman Granz that resulted in the release of fourteen long-playing albums. Granz also recorded Tatum in a myriad of small group settings with such featured artists as Lionel Hampton, Benny Carter, Buddy de Franco, Roy Eldridge, Jo Jones, Buddy Rich, and Ben Webster. The solo piano project however was probably the most ambitious and, considering Granz's intentions, it was only partially successful. According to his liner notes on the original Clef and Verve LPs Granz intended to record and release as many Art Tatum solo selections as possible, thereby building an "Art Tatum library." Most of the tunes were recorded in one take; the producer apparently assumed that his pianist could do no wrong. The end results are always diffuse and uneven because Tatum's health was failing around the time of these sessions. This writer thinks the Norman Granz sessions were more of a token to posterity than an attempt to preserve a finished product. Nevertheless, Tatum's accomplishments are often fascinating. There are times when it seems that Tatum was searching for a new musical language, and some of the startling harmonic and rhythmic complexities in these selections partly indicate that Tatum listened to and had absorbed the innovations of the bop musicians. However, Tatum remained a swing player in his overall conceptions of time and phrasing. Although Tatum played informally with Charlie Parker and other modern musicians one wonders how Tatum's music would have been affected if he had collaborated with these players on a regular basis (as Coleman Hawkins did throughout his career, successfully and uncompromisingly). It is also a pity that, in a project undertaken to preserve huge doses of exceptional pianism, Tatum re-recorded his "semi-classical" arrangements of "Humoresque" and "Elegie" when he could very well have recorded some of the classical piano literature that he knew, such as the Chopin waltzes or the Chopin Prelude in B♭ minor op. 28, No. 16. (There is a private tape existing of Tatum improvising on the Chopin C♯ minor waltz that must be heard to be believed.

Unlike the music making of other major jazz figures, little of Art Tatum's music has been transcribed for publication. There were two books published in the 40s that consisted of one chorus piece edited from longer improvisations and which cannot be considered representative of Tatum's improvisational techniques. A very fine transcription of the 1949 "Aunt Hagar's Blues" is available in John Mehegan's book *Jazz Rhythm and the Improvised Line* (Amsco Music Publishing Company). *Jazz Masters: Art Tatum* is the first book consisting exclusively of complete piano solos transcribed from Art Tatum's released recordings.

The six pieces included herein were recorded between 1938 and 1955 and together display a good representation of Art Tatum's multi-faceted style. The sound quality of the original recordings used for these transcriptions varies from each session. "Ain't Misbehavin' " and "Fine and Dandy" were not originally recorded for commercial release and their sound quality is poor. I have used parentheses encasing 1) certain notes that are not clearly audible but which were possibly played and 2) notes that are not actually played but which are indisputably parts of a musical phrase.

Unfortunately, for transcribers and listeners alike, the remastering of the Norman Granz solo sessions that were reissued on Pablo is extremely poor. The clarity of the bass register is all but totally lost and in general the piano sounds muffled. What one hears on these recent pressings simply cannot compare to the beautifully clear and close-miked piano sound captured on the original Clef and Verve LPs. (To be fair, the sound on *The Tatum Group Masterpieces* is very good.)

Because of divergencies in fingering habits among pianists I have not indicated any fingerings (not wishing to impose my own bad habits!). Some pianists may find many of the left-hand tenths beyond their natural span. Whenever possible one can substitute the right hand for the upper voice of the tenth, or else execute a quick, arpeggiated tenth emphasizing the upper note—a "clipping" device that Tatum often used. As far as realizing a convincing musical interpretation of the notes, when all is said and done, the real essence of this music lies in the original recordings and not in the printed transcriptions. I feel it is more important to emulate the spirit of the music, to aim for a style with a certain kind of sound and phrasing than to try to play every last grace note verbatim. Indeed, if you are so inclined, be encouraged to interpolate your own improvised phrases or runs into these pieces. After all Tatum himself was always making changes here and there in his so-called "set pieces."

Art Tatum's approach to improvisation has fascinated and eluded musicians and critics for years. Compared with his contemporaries Roy Eldridge, Coleman Hawkins, and Teddy Wilson, Tatum was an atavist, a throwback to an older era of jazz pianists. Tatum's method of adhering closely to the melody by use of ornamentation and embellishment comes from James P. Johnson, Fats Waller, and Willie "The Lion" Smith. Like Tatum, who was often accused of playing "set" improvisations, the improvising of Johnson, Waller, and Smith consisted mostly of embellishments and different turns of phrases in the pieces that they played. But it must be remembered that their repertoires mainly consisted of their own elaborately structured multisectioned stride pieces which grew out of the forms that Scott Joplin and Jelly Roll Morton used. Tatum's improvising material almost exclusively consisted of standard Tin Pan Alley songs. By virtue of his extraordinary piano technique and phenomenal ear Tatum created a style that juxtaposed the elegant melodies of Teddy Wilson, the strong rhythmic underpinning of the stride pianists, the rhythmic syncopations and trumpet-like phrases of Earl Hines, and the delicate passage work found in the works of Chopin and Liszt, as well as the popular or semi-classical piano stylists of the day.

It was a style that had a vacillating, mercurial nature with subtley changing pianistic textures and harmonic nuances. For this reason, and also perhaps because it presented something outside of the mainstream of what most jazz musicians were doing, the Tatum style was hard to grasp at first hearing. Yet, his technique and his musicianship meshed together on such a high level that he made everything he played sound easy, and his touch at the keyboard had an elegance and clarity that can easily be compared to the classical pianists Vladimir de Pachmann and Alfred Cortot and that, in jazz, only his mentor Fats Waller could match.

Notes on the Solos

Ain't Misbehavin' (1938)

This recording is a good introduction to the Art Tatum style. The opening chorus contains all his stylistic traits using different registers in an orchestral way, paraphrasing the melody with runs, alternating walking tenths with stride passages, and occasionally using reharmonizations. One significant aspect of Tatum's use of left-hand tenths is the way he "clips" or shortens the bass note, leaving his thumb on the upper note (see measures 1, 2, 4, 24). This technique is explicitly used in the opening and in the last chorus of "Moonglow."

Notice how Tatum uses pure melodic phrases in the transitory measures before the beginning of the following A or B sections of the tune (measures 7-8, 15-16, 23-24, 31-32). The bridge is the point of greatest harmonic tension. In contrast to the chromatic movement of the bass line in the A section the root and third remain stationary while the fifth chromatically ascends to the major sixth and again rises to the seventh along with the third forming a dominant seventh chord that unexpectedly resolves to a V_6 chord. Tatum takes advantage of this structure by fashioning a stoptime chorus each time. The first time through he keeps the melody virtually intact, the second bridge is much louder, engulfed with thick chords and brash octaves and the third time it is quieter, with elaborate right-hand runs and embellishments totally replacing the melody (for how many times do we need to hear it?). Tatum's deft use of musical quotation is characterized in the unexpected ending where "Turkey in the Straw" is turned into a cleverly reharmonized II-V-I sequence.

Fine and Dandy (1941)

This is perhaps the most revealing of all Art Tatum recordings. In this rare document of Tatum playing in one of those legendary Harlem after-hours clubs, we find his playing to be leaner in texture and completely uncluttered. This is, no doubt, partially due to the deficiencies of the out-of-tune, beat-up piano and the presence of the time-keeping whiskbrooms player.

In reading through these transcriptions one notices Tatum's frequent use of grace notes, trills, tremolos, and blues licks (patterns using the flatted intervals of the 3rd, 5th, and 7th degrees of the major scale). What sets this version of "Fine and Dandy" apart from his other recordings of standards is that Tatum uses these "bluesy" embellishments as structural cornerstones for the four improvised choruses following the statement of the theme. He takes full advantage of the whiskbrooms, indulging himself in some telling stop-time passages that are interspersed with intricate right-hand phrases, not unlike the solo work of Earl Hines. Indeed, the Hines influence is apparent throughout this recording.

Although this piece is as full of stylistic juxtapositions as any of his other recordings, Tatum's unique fusion of blues, classical piano literature, extended harmonic patterns, and straight-ahead swing is particularly successful here. There is a structural momentum that builds throughout each chorus based upon the chord voicings and rhythmic patterns set up in the thematic exposition and the stark first chorus (measures 39-40).

The embellished F riff (measures 39-42) appears in different forms and functions throughout the piece, most notably at the beginning of the second chorus (measures 71-80), the beginning of the third chorus, in the form of a trill (measures 103-112), and in the syncopated left-hand pattern in the second part of the third chorus (measures 120-127). Tatum frequently begins phrases, introduces new ideas, and changes the pianistic texture on the weak beats of a measure, thereby giving the material at hand a smoother flow and creating a more flexible, transparent interplay between the right and left hands. Note, for example, how the swinging right-hand line in measures 57-58 actually begins on the upbeat of the bar, with the walking bass starting a bit later and then stopping abruptly to let the right-hand run continue alone, only to be resolved by jabbing left-hand chords in measures 60-61 which in turn prepare for another stop-time passage. The new material introduced at the beginning of the first four choruses begins at least one bar beforehand, thereby creating greater continuity between choruses.

In the penultimate chorus, the melody is restated in the style of the opening, with some altered harmonies (measures 154-164) that serve as a deceptive ending, then Tatum suddenly lets loose with a loud, two-handed blues run that leads right into the last chorus, where he repeats the same procedure (measures 185-195), restating the melody and suddenly bursting into a bluesy stride passage. This leads into a stop-time coda which is a pretty harmonic sequence based on the last four bars of the theme that humorously revolves with a two-bar blues phrase. Another interesting structural feature is the way the second eight bars of the theme are restated in each chorus in right-hand octaves and walking tenth chords in the left hand. These chords are harmonized differently each time and the melody also has different rhythmic embellishments.

In "Fine and Dandy," Art Tatum created multi-leveled variations on a theme in which the separateness of the thematic components is maintained by the way they are individually developed throughout the piece. Yet, due to Tatum's innate sense of proportion and balance, there is an organic unity embracing these disparate elements, enabling them to co-exist in a larger structure that transcends the confines of the thirty-two bar song form.

Moonglow (1955)

This little masterpiece captures Tatum in an eloquently reckless mood. The subtle harmonic shifts present in the walking left-hand chords slip by so fast that they tickle the ear, the characteristic runs take on unexpected turns (measures 62-66 are particularly delicious), and it seems as though no matter what kind of trap Tatum falls into he works himself out of it quickly and painlessly (see measures 47-48, 80-81, and 87-89 for such traps). Tatum's *clipped-bass note* technique is effectively used in the exposition of the theme (measures 9-19) and in the third chorus (measures 106-121); the latter measures are notable for Tatum's imaginative reharmonization of the theme.

I Surrender, Dear (1955)

Of all the components making up the Art Tatum style it is the art of ad lib playing that is at once easy to approach pianistically yet musically very difficult to pull off. Tatum created an excellent model for out-of-tempo solo piano playing that can serve as a strong vehicle for expressive, lyrical, and virtuosic music making in the hands of a skilled and sensitive pianist-musician.

In ballads, he would play the theme ad libitum, often exploring different ways of altering and revoicing the harmony. He would then use the last few bars of the theme to establish his tempo and execute a number of choruses. Toward the end of the piece he would again play out of tempo, either restating or paraphrasing the theme and then would finish with a little coda. When Tatum played tunes with an AABA structure he would close the improvisation by repeating the B and the final A sections of the tune.

"I Surrender, Dear" is a fine example of Art Tatum's ballad approach, although he really does not play ad lib until the last five measures of the piece. In this particular selection Tatum states the theme in tempo. The first sixteen bars are executed in a manner akin to classical piano styles in that the rhythmic focus is centered within the highly ornamented treatment of the melody in the right hand and in the connective runs. Tatum frequently follows sections of tender passage work with thick arpeggiated chords and he makes effective use of left-hand counter-melodies and decorative harmonic embellishments such as the whole tone scale in measures 18 and 20.

An important and revealing aspect of Tatum's ballad style, in relation to his recordings of 1949 and after, is found in the way he constantly wavers from a "straight," non-dotted, even rhythmic pulse to triplets or dotted eighths and sixteenths, of a standard jazz pulse—often within the same bar (measures 38-39 and 73-81; See Sweet Lorraine II). This technique illustrates Tatum's romantic impulses and there are many other tunes that utilize this vacillating rhythmic approach in the Norman Granz solo sessions (these include such tunes as "Lover Come Back to Me," "You're Blase," "In a Sentimental Mood," "Don't Worry About Me," "The Way You Look Tonight," "That Old Feeling," "Memories of You," "Danny Boy," and "Jitterbug Waltz"). Indeed, Tatum would sometimes rhapsodize at length before safely settling into jazz tempo.

Sweet Lorraine I (Decca, 1940)
Sweet Lorraine II (Capitol, 1949)

Because of his penchant for setting his improvisations into arrangements Art Tatum was often accused of not being a *real* jazz musician. It is true that Tatum could reproduce some of his recorded interpretations note for note. (His Pablo recordings of "Yesterdays" and "Begin the Beguine" are not only virtual reproductions of early recordings but they also bear out the old jazz credo stating that "familiarity breeds faster tempos." Having heard most of Tatum's complete recordings, commercial and non-commercial alike including many re-recordings of standard tunes, I think it's instructive to take different recordings of one common tune and compare them chronologically. Not only did Tatum improvise with the melodic and harmonic materials of these songs but he also improvised with the structure of his so-called "arrangements." For example, the basic arrangement of the 1940 version of "Get Happy" is similar to the lesser known transcription disc version from 1939. Within one year Tatum's approach to the tune evolved significantly. The later, commercially issued version is more balanced, the relationships of ideas from chorus to chorus are clearer and, most importantly, Tatum has added a long introduction that sets the mood for the piece and embraces the essential structure of the song so when he finally arrives at the theme the basic arrangement makes a little more sense.

Likewise, the 1940 version of "Sweet Lorraine" is fuller in its realization than its earlier counterpart (also taken from a transcription disc). The harmonic sequence at measure 7 is smoother in the later version. It is basically a vi V I IV progression with contrapuntal movement in sevenths and tenths, whereas the earlier version has what is basically an augmented sixth chord on the third and fourth beats of measure 7 resolving to a dominant chord that lasts all of measure 8. The sequence on the later recording resolves to the tonic instead. The introduction to the piece is now four measures instead of two, again representing a more balanced revision.

There is much to be said about Art Tatum's landmark 1940 recording of

"Sweet Lorraine." It has a sparse, lyrical quality that meshes perfectly with the gentle swing style and the effective, medium-tempo, full-chorded stride passages with their "clipped" tenths and subtle countermelodies. Tatum's runs are naturally developed from melodic impulses and are used in such a discreet manner that they are even singable. Tatum's harmonic genius is revealed as much in his melody line as in his chord progressions. The contours of these lines are fascinating; they are perpetually spiced with unusual intervals and telling accents (see measures 11-12, 43-44, 75-76, and the quote from "The Monkey Wrapped His Tail Around the Flagpole" at measures 67-8). Note also how Tatum changes the harmony each time around on the last two measures of the bridge, reaching a climax at measures 59-60 going into the last eight measures. (In later recordings Tatum played these measures of the bridge with the same harmony as in the previous eight measures, thereby repeating the same sequence of chromatically descending seventh chords—give or take a few augmented alterations.)

By contrast, "Sweet Lorraine II" is glib, carefree, and rhythmically and harmonically more complex, if not as totally organized as the earlier version. Tatum utilizes more sophisticated bass lines and walking left-hand chords, a major characteristic of his later work. Note his inventive use of quoting, this time from the Paderewski "Minuet in G," "Waiting for the Robert E. Lee," and Ethelbert Nevin's "Narcissus."

Ain't Misbehavin'

Razaf
Waller
Brooks

♩=118-120 Tempo slows down toward the end.

15

16

18

Fine and Dandy

Paul Jones
Kay Swift

33

Moonglow

Delange
Mills
Hudson

I Surrender Dear

Gordon Clifford
Harry Barris

46

49

intended

53

Sweet Lorraine (I)

Parish
Burwell

Sweet Lorraine (II)

Parish
Burwell
transcribed by Felicity Howlett

A Selected Discography

Art Tatum . . . "On The Air"
Aircheck 21
(features his first solo recording, "Tiger Rag" and airchecks from 1934-1945)

Piano Starts Here
Columbia CS 9655
(Four 1933 recordings and the May 1949 "Just Jazz" Concert, Shrine
    Auditorium, Los Angeles)

Tatum Is Art
Musidisc/Jazz Anthology 30 JA 5177 (French)
(Piano solos from 1938 and 1939)

Get Happy!
Black Lion BLP 30194 (British)
Standard Transcriptions Q126 and Q135, from 1938-9, includes "Ain't
    Misbehavin' ")

Art Tatum Masterpieces
MCA 2-4019
(includes "Sweet Lorraine")

Art Tatum Masterpieces Volume 2 and James P. Johnson Plays Fats Waller
MCA 2-4112

God Is In The House
Onyx 205 Musidisc/Jazz Anthology 30 JA 5111 (French)
(1940-41 Harlem After-Hours Sessions, includes "Fine and Dandy")

Song of the Vagabonds
Black Lion BLP 30166 (British)
(includes the complete 1945 ARA sessions)

Solo Piano
Capitol M-11028
(1949 sessions, includes "Sweet Lorraine")

The Tatum Solo Masterpieces
Pablo 13 LP set 2625 703
(1953-55 recordings, includes "Moonglow" and "I Surrender, Dear")

The Tatum Group Masterpieces
Pablo 8 LP set 2625 708

The Complete Art Tatum Piano Discoveries
Twentieth Century-Fox TCF 102-2S
(Private party recordings from 1956)